AIRCRAFT CARRIERS

Modern Military Techniques

MODERN MILITARY TECHNIQUES
AIRCRAFT CARRIERS

Antony Preston

Illustrations by
Tony Gibbons • Peter Sarson • Tony Bryan

Lerner Publications Company • Minneapolis

This book is available in two editions:
Library binding by Lerner Publications Company
Soft cover by First Avenue Editions
241 First Avenue North
Minneapolis, Minnesota 55401

Library of Congress Cataloging in Publication Data

Preston, Antony, 1938-
　　Aircraft carriers.

　　(Modern military techniques)
　　Previously published as: Carriers. c1984.
　　Includes index.
　　Summary: Traces the history of aircraft carriers
since 1914, chronicling the role played by these ships
in World War II and in modern defense systems.
　　1. Aircraft carriers—Juvenile literature. 2. Am-
phibious assault ships—Juvenile literature. 3. Naval
battle groups—Juvenile literature. [1. Aircraft car-
riers. 2. Ships—History. 3. Naval art and science]
I. Gibbons, Tony, ill. II. Sarson, Peter, ill.
III. Bryan, Tony, ill. IV. Title. V. Series.
V874.P74 1985　　　　359.3′255　　　　84-9669
ISBN 0-8225-1377-3 (lib. bdg.)
ISBN 0-8225-9504-4 (pbk.)

Manufactured in the United States of America

4　5　6　7　8　9　10　93　92　91　90　89　88　87　86

CONTENTS

1 Early Seaplane Carriers

The first seaplane carriers were fast cross-Channel passenger steamers with big cranes and canvas hangars at the after-end of the ship. The hangars gave some protection to the flimsy seaplanes from wind and rain, but the early seaplanes were easily damaged by waves as well. In October 1914, HMS *Engadine* and HMS *Riviera* tried to launch an attack on the coast of Germany, but all six seaplanes were unable to get airborne.

Two months later, three seaplane carriers tried to repeat the raid. But although seven out of nine Short seaplanes got into the air, they could not find the airship sheds which they were trying to bomb. More raids followed in 1915 but failed each time because of bad weather. During the battle of Jutland, one of the *Engadine's* seaplanes sighted the German Fleet, but her radio broke down.

In a typical operation, as shown here, the seaplanes were wheeled out of the hangar, their wings were unfolded, and the crane then lifted them into the water. If they took off and returned safely, the pilots would then taxi alongside to allow the seaplanes to be hoisted back on board.

All these crude pioneering aircraft carriers suffered from having to operate inefficient aircraft. Later in the First World War, some ships were given runways to allow them to fly off wheeled

landplanes instead of the clumsy seaplanes. But their attempts to bomb land bases were almost useless. Their best achievement was to provide reconnaissance for long-range bombardment, but they pointed the way to future developments.

A typical early seaplane carrier of the Royal Navy was HMS *Engadine*. Formerly a South Eastern & Chatham Railway steamer, built in 1911, she could steam at 22½ knots, a speed that would enable her to keep up with the battlefleet. She was taken over by the Navy in August 1914 and went to Chatham to be converted. Nearly 132 feet (40m) of the after deck was cleared of obstructions, and a wooden deck was built to carry three seaplanes. The hangar was merely a canvas cover stretched on frames over this deck.

The ship was given Navy radio and signalling equipment, a gasoline tank, and a bomb-magazine, while two 4-inch and a 6-pounder anti-aircraft gun gave her some chance of defending herself against attack.

After the Armistice in November 1918, the *Engadine* was stripped of all her wartime fittings and returned to her owners. In the 1930s, the railway company sold her to a Filipino operator, who renamed her *Corregidor.* In December 1941, the old ship hit a Japanese mine and sank in Manila Bay.

Left: HMS *Engadine*

Right: HMS *Empress*

2 Runways and Catapults

Even before the first seaplane carriers were converted in 1914, experiments had been made to operate aircraft from ships. In November 1910, Eugene Ely flew a Curtiss Pusher biplane off a wooden platform built over the bows of the light cruiser USS *Birmingham*. Just two months later, Ely went one better and landed on a similar platform built over the stern of the armored cruiser USS *Pennsylvania*. The aircraft had a wheeled undercarriage, but as there were no brakes, there was a simple arrangement of 22 wires stretched across the deck to catch hooks on the plane's undercarriage.

After Eugene Ely's successful takeoff and landing, the US Navy developed catapults, mechanical devices capable of "accelerating" an aircraft to a safe takeoff speed. In October 1915, the armored cruiser USS *North Carolina* was fitted with a catapult on her quarterdeck. When it proved successful, two more cruisers were fitted with them.

The Royal Navy chose a different solution. In 1915 several small cruisers were fitted with a sloping wooden ramp over the bow to allow a wheeled Sopwith Pup fighter aircraft to take off. Unlike seaplanes, the Pup and its successor, the Camel, had sufficient speed and rate of climb to engage Zeppelin airships, which constantly gave away the position of British warships. So successful were these platforms that by 1918 the majority of battleships were fitted to fly aircraft off their gun turrets.

The first successful war-flight from a ship was made from the seaplane carrier HMS *Vindex*. On November 3, 1915, a Bristol C-type Scout biplane took off from a ramp built over the ship's bows. To allow the aircraft to be recovered, flotation bags were lashed to the undercarriage. As a result, when the pilot landed alongside the *Vindex,* he and his aircraft could be hoisted in by crane.

In June 1917, a Sopwith Pup fighter was successfully flown off the forecastle of the light cruiser HMS *Yarmouth,* using a platform only 20 feet (6m) long. Light aircraft like the Pup could take off when the ship was steaming at 20 knots, using the wind over the deck to get airborne. Subsequently, another pilot was able to take off from the *Yarmouth* and shoot down a Zeppelin, proof that these enormous airships could be countered.

A Sopwith 1½-Strutter takes off from a platform over the twin barrels of a 12 inch gun turret.

A Fairey seaplane perched on an experimental catapult mounted on the hopper barge HMS *Slinger* in 1918

Left: Eugene Ely's Curtiss Pusher rolling down the ramp over the bows of the scout cruiser USS *Birmingham* in November 1910

3
Improvements in Landing

First World War, a great effort was made to cure the problems.

Both the British and the Americans experimented with systems of parallel wires down the length of the flight deck. In theory, the wires would steady the aircraft until it slowed down by means of the landing hooks on the aircraft's undercarriage. This was not effective, as it did nothing to stop the aircraft pitching over on its nose. But it remained in use during the 1920s.

The best solution was produced by the Americans and then copied by the Japanese, but it was first tried in 1917. The aircraft was fitted with

All the early attempts at landing aircraft on ships were highly dangerous. The light aircraft were likely to be caught by gusts of wind. Out of control, they would either crash on the deck or swerve over the side. Whatever happened, the pilot was very likely to be killed. Therefore, after the end of the

Left: The first successful arresting gear used a sting hook retracted under the tail until the aircraft was ready to land. Hydraulic gear slowed down the rate at which the wire pulled out, bringing the aircraft to a stop.

a retractable hook under the tail, known as a "sting hook" as it resembled the sting of a wasp. Several widely-spaced wires were stretched from side to side, and, when the aircraft landed, the tail-hook would almost certainly engage one of the wires. All that was needed was to strengthen the tail structure of the aircraft and to provide a strong barrier at the forward end of the flight deck in case all the wires were missed.

This so-called "arrestor wire" system became standard in all navies' aircraft carriers and is still in use today.

The American *Essex* class had the most unusual arrangement of arrestor wires. When the design was drawn up in the late 1930s, the specification called for aircraft to be capable of landing at either end. The idea behind this unusual request seems to have been that the ship might be damaged at one end but still be capable of operating her aircraft — a set of circumstances which never occurred.

The flight deck of the *Essex*, therefore, had two groups of arrestor wires, one in the normal position and a second group further forward. To make such an arrangement work, it was essential that the ship could steam backwards at a comparatively high speed. This set the designers a difficult task, as warships usually steam very slowly in reverse.

The arrangement was tried at least once. Photographs taken in 1942 show an aircraft landing over the stern of the *Essex*. But later ships had the extra arrestor wires removed.

Top right: The USS *Langley* tried longitudinal wires based on British ideas, but they caused as many accidents as they prevented.

Bottom right: The *Langley's* arrestor system was changed to athwartship wires, a great improvement that has since become standard.

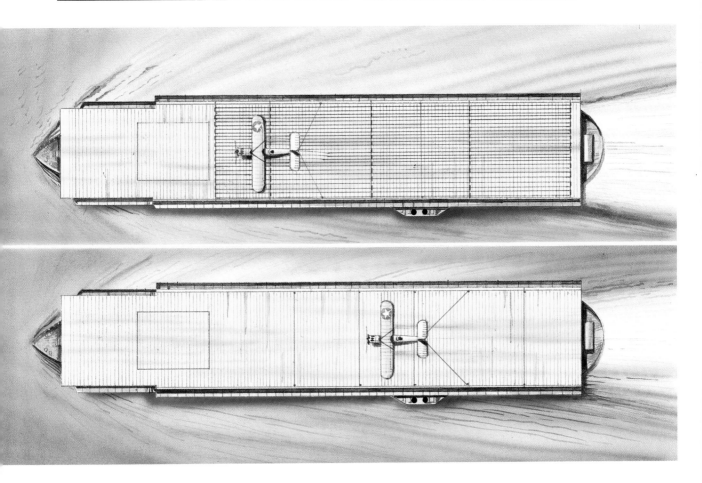

4 Hangar Design

Early hangars had been no more than light structures intended to keep wind and rain off the aircraft. But after the First World War, much more thought was given to the design of the second generation of aircraft carriers.

When converting the *Lexington* and *Saratoga* from battlecruisers into carriers, the US Navy chose an open-design hangar that extended to the sides of the hull. This had the great benefit of permitting the maximum number of aircraft to be carried, and any gasoline fumes could be easily dispersed by ventilating the hangar. The most notable feature of an open hangar, therefore, became large openings in the hull sides, which were closed by roller shutters in rough weather. To permit a through draught, it would only be necessary to open some of the shutters, although there was a proper system of ventilators as well.

The Japanese naval air command followed American ideas and built most of its carriers with open hangars. The British, on the other hand, were worried about the high risk of fire, and to combat this developed something quite different. The so-called "closed hangar" was not only separated from the sides of the ship by workshops and other compartments but was also given its own separate ventilation. This was an essential part of a closed hangar, for the enclosed box hangar needed to be emptied of gasoline fumes as fast as possible.

The Royal Navy's carriers suffered throughout

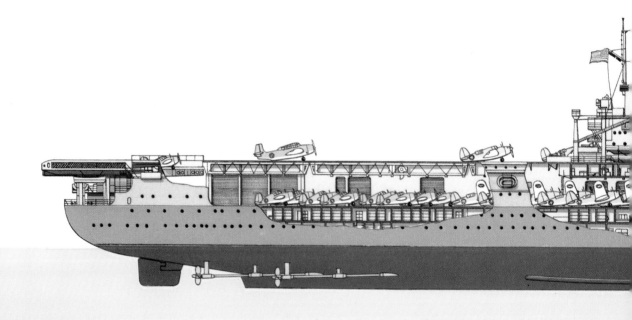

the Second World War from small numbers of aircraft. But off Okinawa in 1945, they proved much better able to survive hangar fires than either Japanese or American carriers. No British-designed carrier was lost by a hangar fire throughout the war.

The fate of the USS *Franklin* is a graphic illustration of the horror of a big gasoline explosion aboard a carrier. On March 19, 1945, she and the rest of Task Force 58 flew air strikes against the Japanese mainland. During this operation, the *Franklin* was hit by two 250kg bombs that landed on the flight deck.

The hangar was not penetrated, but fuel from the aircraft on deck and from fuel lines underneath caught fire and spread to spare bombs and rockets. The *Franklin's* hull and machinery were undamaged, but the suffocating smoke from the fires in the hangar was drawn into the main ventilation system. The majority of the 724 dead and 265 wounded were suffocated by fumes and

smoke, many of them in compartments far from the fire.

Although the *Franklin's* crew extinguished the fires and got the ship back to San Francisco, the ship was never fully operational again.

The drawing shows a longitudinal section through the USS *Yorktown* (CV.5) built at Newport News Shipyard, Virginia, and completed in 1937. With an overall length of 808.5 feet (245 meters), the *Yorktown* had a displacement, when fully loaded, of 25,500 tons. The open-type hangar could hold 80 aircraft, or four squadrons of 18 aircraft each, together with supplies and extra fighters. Aircraft were moved by means of the three center line elevators. In addition, there were ship's catapults to launch the aircraft directly from the hangar deck (though these were never used in practice). Able to steam at 33 knots, the *Yorktown* was highly maneuverable, and the general design became standard for American carriers. The USS *Yorktown* was sunk on June 6, 1942, at Midway.

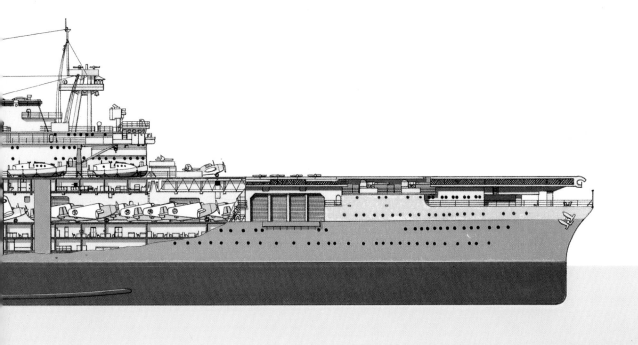

5
Pearl Harbor

The Japanese attack on the US Navy's main fleet base at Pearl Harbor in Hawaii was one of the most devastating events of modern naval history. Six Japanese aircraft carriers launched 129 dive bombers, 143 torpedo bombers, and 132 fighters against the heavily defended base on December 7, 1941. In two separate strikes, Admiral Nagumo's superbly trained aircrews sank four battleships, disabled four more, and wiped out numerous aircraft on the ground.

The Americans had unwisely counted on the shallowness of the anchorage to protect their ships from air-launched torpedoes. But the Japanese countered this by fitting each torpedo with a special wooden tail to ensure that it did not dive too deep. With seven of the battleships tightly packed in "Battleship Row," the Japanese had little trouble identifying their targets. Apart from sporadic ground anti-aircraft fire, there was little to distract them from the task of aiming bombs and torpedoes.

And yet Pearl Harbor was not the decisive battle that the Japanese had wanted. Quite apart from the miscalculation that America would be too shocked to retaliate, the Japanese intelligence was faulty. As a result, they failed to attack the most important target. Poor intelligence prevented Admiral Nagumo from learning that the all-important aircraft carriers of the US Pacific Fleet were away from Pearl Harbor. The battleships could be replaced by others from the Atlantic, but the carriers could not. If the repair shops and, above all, the oil storage tanks had been destroyed, Pearl Harbor would have been unusable for a year or more. As it was, all but two of the battleships were salvaged and returned to service.

Three days after the attack on Pearl Harbor,

the British capital ships *Prince of Wales* and *Repulse* were sunk off the coast of Malaya by Japanese torpedo bombers. This disaster, coupled with the Pearl Harbor attack, effectively ended the dominance of the battleship. Previously it had been hoped that by increasing the thickness of deck armor and adding numbers of heavy anti-aircraft guns, battleships would be able to defend themselves against air attack. The battleships sunk at Pearl Harbor were all elderly ships, designed 20-25 years before and modernized. But HMS *Prince of Wales* was a brand-new battleship, incorporating all the latest ideas for anti-aircraft defense, including radar control and a new design of high-angled gun.

Experience was to show that, if provided with adequate air support, the battleship still had a useful role to play, and that even the aircraft carrier needed the support of other ships if she was to survive heavy attack.

In the Japanese attack on Pearl Harbor on December 7, 1941, the two waves approached from the north at 7:40 AM and 8:50 AM. The first wave, which achieved complete surprise, attacked and neutralized Haleiwa and Wheeler airfields on the way in before attacking the ships in the main anchorage.

From the northwest, one section attacked a line which included the light cruisers *Detroit* and *Raleigh,* the target ship *Utah,* and the seaplane tender *Tangier.* A detachment attacked the docks on the south side of the anchorage, sinking three destroyers and damaging the battleship *Pennsylvania.*

The main strike came in over the southeastern part of the anchorage, heading for Battleship Row off Ford Island. Here the most destruction took place: the sinking of the battleships *California, Oklahoma, Arizona, Tennessee, West Virginia,* and *Maryland.* A detachment from this group also struck further to the south, over Hickam Field, and sank the mine-layer *Oglala.*

The first wave comprised 49 high-level bombers, 40 torpedo-bombers, 51 dive-bombers, and 43 fighters. The second wave was made up of 54 high-level bombers, 78 dive-bombers, and 35 fighters.

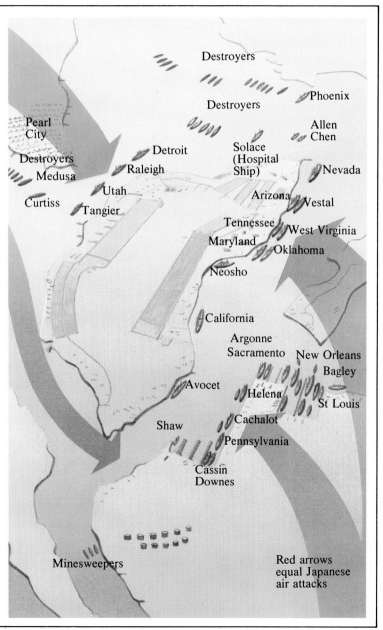

15

6 Escort Carriers, MAC-Ships, and CAM-Ships

Towards the end of 1940, the Germans began to use their long-range Fw200 Kondor bombers to attack British shipping in the Western Approaches and to provide intelligence for the U-Boats. To counter this threat, the Admiralty converted five merchantmen to Catapult-Armed Merchant ships (CAM-Ships), putting a catapult on the forecastle. Each CAM-Ship carried a single Hurricane fighter, which was launched as soon as the Fw200 Kondor appeared. It was an expensive way of shooting down bombers, for each time the Hurricane came down in the water, the pilot had to wait in his inflatable dinghy until a ship picked him up.

As early as 1938, the Admiralty had considered "trade protection carriers" or converted mechant ships, and the idea was revived in 1941. Two prototypes were built, one in the United States and one in Britain, and the USS *Long Island* and HMS *Audacity* were in service before the end of that year. They proved so successful that many more were built.

The most important area in which these "escort carriers" operated was the so-called "Black Gap" in the mid-Atlantic, where shorebased aircraft could not reach. By allowing each convoy to take aircraft with it, the escort carrier provided continuous air support through this "Black Gap" and neutralized the U-Boats.

The Merchant Aircraft Carrier (MAC-Ship) was a stopgap idea produced in Britain while the escort carriers were being built. A group of tankers and grain carriers were given flight decks. But unlike the escort carriers, they carried their original cargo and were manned by civilian crews.

The first British escort carrier, HMS *Audacity*, was an ex-German prize: the banana boat *Hannover*, captured in 1940. For her conversion, she was stripped to the upper deck and a wooden flight was added. There was no time to provide a hangar and elevator, and so the six Martlet II (Wildcat) fighters were parked on the flight deck. The ship was steered from a small navigating position on the starboard side of the flight deck, right forward.

The *Audacity* was an immediate success. In only three convoy actions, her Martlet IIs succeeded in shooting down, damaging, or driving off an estimated 200 Fw200 Kondors. Her brief career came to an end in December 1941 when she was torpedoed during a particularly fierce convoy battle. But in only four months, she had proved that many more escort carriers were needed. By 1945 the escort carrier, or CVE, had become much more than a stopgap and was being used to support amphibious landings.

The most sophisticated version of the escort carrier was the British light fleet carrier. Displacing 14,000 tons and built to mercantile standards up to the main deck, the *Colossus* class could operate 48 aircraft and steam at 24½ knots. Performance and dimensions were carefully worked out after war experience showed that the big carriers rarely needed to steam at full speed. The design was kept simple to permit them to be built by non-specialist shipyards. Only three were completed at the end of the Second World War, but they saw widespread post-war service, notably in the Korean War. Many

---

Top: The escort carrier (CVE) was a miniature carrier, with hangar and catapult, built on a mercantile hull, usually on the stocks.
Center: The MAC-Ship was a bulk grain-carrier or oil-tanker with a flight deck added; her aircraft were housed below the flight deck, but she carried cargo as well.
Bottom: The CAM-Ship was merely a merchant ship with a catapult on the forecastle.

---

were transferred to other navies, including those of France, Holland, Australia, and Canada. Because the design allowed for "stretch," they were constantly reconstructed and modernized to take heavier aircraft. The most outstanding example was the Argentine Navy's flagship *Vienticinco de Mayo* (ex-Dutch *Karel Doorman*, ex-HMS *Venerable*). Armed with air-launched Exocet missiles, she has been modernized to operate Super Etendard strike aircraft.

Hangar   Officers' quarters   Ward room   Exhaust   Bridge

Single prop

Balanced rudder   Stores hold   Engines   Machine area   Galley bar   Stores

7
The Angled Deck

Although the carrier had proved itself as the new capital ship, the introduction of jet aircraft in 1945 caused many problems. All the early jet fighters and fighter-bombers were sluggish in handling and used much fuel, and it was feared that their landing speeds might be too high for carriers.

The British, with smaller carriers than the Americans, looked at a number of solutions. In 1952 HMS *Triumph* tried out an experimental angled landing deck with arrestor wires left in the original position. Aircraft then did "touch-and-go" landings to test the effect of landing 10 degrees off the carrier's centerline. After similar tests in the United States, the carrier *Antietam* was fully converted. Her flight deck was angled out by 8 degrees. The ship carried out 4000 deck-landings, proving that the angled deck was much safer; today it remains standard.

The advantage of the angled deck is that it allows a pilot who misses an arrestor wire to accelerate away and come around for a second landing. Before, if he missed the wire, he had to be prevented from crashing into the "deck park" of aircraft waiting to fly off the forward end of the deck. Although nylon safety nets caused less damage to the aircraft than the old-style barriers, barrier-crashes were still the major cause of casualties. Another advantage is that more of the forward area can be used for aircraft movements, even when aircraft are landing, which speeds up flying operations.

The post-war experiments that led up to the angled deck included an even more unusual solution: the flexible deck. In 1948 HMS *Warrior* had a platform built on her flight deck, supporting large flexible air-filled rubber bags.

The first aircraft to use the new system was a Sea Vampire jet fighter, which landed with its undercarriage retracted. The idea behind the flexible deck was to eliminate the weight of undercarriage and tail-hook and to have a safer "pancake" landing without all the risks of an arrested landing.

The flexible landing deck was successful, but it had to be dropped because it would have meant that all shore-based airfields would have had to be re-equipped with the gear. One of the principal advantages of carrier aircraft is that they can operate from shore bases without any difficulty, and it was felt that this should not be sacrificed.

In US Navy carriers of the 1960s, the deck-edge aircraft elevator was left in the uppermost position, where it formed an extension to the angled deck. This arrangement proved so useful that it was made permanent, and the deck-edge elevator was relocated on the starboard side aft. The standard technique is to land at full throttle, but with air brakes extended to reduce landing-speed. This makes for tricky handling but ensures that if the sting hook misses the wire, the pilot can accelerate and take off again. If throttled back, he would run the risk of stalling and falling off the end of the deck into the sea. All modern aircraft carriers use some form of angled deck, even ships like the

---

The first carrier to have a full angled deck was the later *Essex* class USS *Antietam* (CV-36), which was converted in 1952-53. She proved ideal for the conversion as her main defensive armament, four twin 5 in. gun mountings, was grouped forward and aft of the island, leaving the port side comparatively uncluttered. After 4000 safe landings aboard the *Antietam,* the new system became standard for American carriers. In today's super carriers, the angled deck sponson is wide enough to accommodate an additional pair of steam catapults.

Soviet *Kiev* class and the British *Invincible* and *Illustrious*, which operate vertical short takeoff and landing (V/STOL) aircraft and helicopters. The reason is that the Yak-36 Forger and the Sea Harrier benefit from a rolling takeoff to improve performance. A refinement of the angled deck is the "Alaska Highway" provided in ships like HMS *Hermes*. An extension on the starboard side, outboard of the island superstructure, permits aircraft to be moved backwards and forwards without interrupting flying operations.

The decision to include angled decks did not cause too many difficulties for designers, for the extra weight of the deck and its supporting sponson helped to offset the weight of the island on the port side. This weight had previously been offset by additional oil fuel carried on the port side below the waterline. The main drawback was that anti-aircraft gun positions had to be moved elsewhere to make room for the extension.

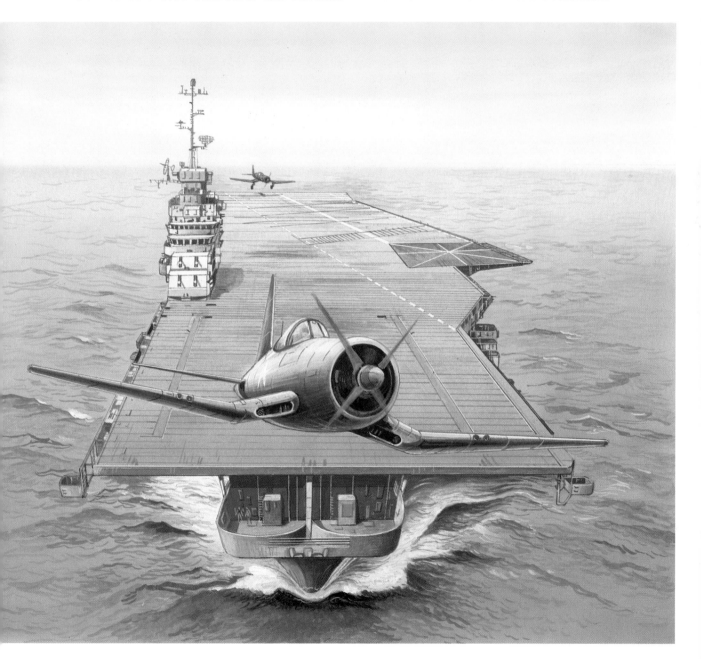

8 Mirror Landing Sights

At the time the angled deck was under development, another British team was designing an automatic landing aid. Previously, an incoming pilot was informed about such things as his height above the deck and angle of wings from a landing control officer or "batsman." Using a pair of "paddles" (with lights for night-landings), the batsman signalled "too low," "too high," "left wing down" or, if the pilot did not get it right, a "waveoff." However, as landing speeds became higher and higher, the batsmen proved less able to judge the approach of the aircraft. By 1949 it was clear that some mechanical method must be found.

Legend has it that a British officer used his secretary's lipstick and mirror to enable him to guide his chin down to the desk-top. But whatever the origins, the "mirror landing sight" became a reality in 1952. It used a row of parallel lights focused into a mirror to produce a pattern that is only visible to a pilot coming in at the right height and with his wings level. Today the system has been greatly refined, with fresnel lenses providing a clearer pattern of lights, and the system is used as a back-up to electronically aided devices in the aircraft.

The normal position for landing lights is at the port side of the after end of the flight deck, where

they can be seen most easily by the pilot of an incoming aircraft.

The flight deck of a modern carrier is a bewildering mixture of noise and movement. Modern high-performance aircraft, such as the US Navy's F-14 Tomcat or the French Super Etendard, do not handle well at very low speed, and so the technique of landing requires them to come in using considerable power with air brakes extended. This allows them to accelerate off the deck if the tail-hook does not engage one of the cross-deck wires. During a normal landing, the tail-hook engages and the arrestor wire runs out through pulleys on the deck. To avoid stretching this wire to breaking-point, the pilot must cut his engines immediately.

The landing light system is essential during the approach as it ensures that the pilot holds his aircraft at the best angle to catch an arrestor wire. It is not for nothing that pilots call a deck landing a "slowed-down crash."

The pilot landing on an aircraft carrier sees the fresnel lenses of the landing sight, which tell him that he is at the right height above the deck and his wings are level. In addition, he has audio signals to warn him if his speed is dropping. If the pilot is landing at the right angle, he sees a horizontal bar across the projector that is high if he is too high or low if he is too low. The horizontal lights offer him a datum line, and there are also red lights for a wave-off if the landing has to be aborted for any reason. In today's American carriers, the lenses are controlled from the "Pri-fly" control position high up in the island superstructure. This reduces the needed number of deck personnel.

9 Steam Catapults

Undoubtedly the biggest advance in naval aviation after 1945 was the invention of the steam catapult. During the war, carrier aircraft became so heavy that by 1945 very few of them could do a conventional "free" takeoff, and catapult launches became standard. The post-war generation of aircraft were even heavier, to the point where existing catapults could not cope.

Under the guidance of Commander C. C. Mitchell RNVR, the Royal Navy produced the steam catapult that used steam from the ship's boilers. In principle, there are two parallel slotted cylinders, and steam drives pistons down each cylinder. The secret lies in a special launching valve which regulates the thrust of the catapult according to the weight of each aircraft, admitting only sufficient steam to launch it at the correct speed.

The aircraft is attached to a sliding hook on deck by means of a "bridle," which falls clear when the aircraft becomes airborne. The steam catapult has sufficient power to launch an aircraft while the carrier is lying at anchor, and its power

Catapult System

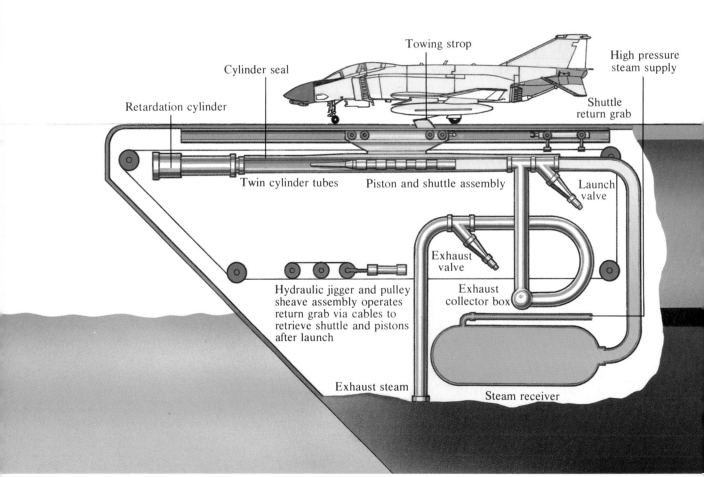

Towing strop

Cylinder seal

High pressure steam supply

Retardation cylinder

Shuttle return grab

Twin cylinder tubes

Piston and shuttle assembly

Launch valve

Exhaust valve

Hydraulic jigger and pulley sheave assembly operates return grab via cables to retrieve shuttle and pistons after launch

Exhaust collector box

Exhaust steam

Steam receiver

can be increased to cope with any aircraft in the foreseeable future.

The first warship fitted with a steam catapult was HMS *Perseus* in 1951. After a demonstration, the US Navy ordered them to be fitted in the USS *Hancock*. Her first steam catapult launch took place in June 1954. Since that time, it has been standard in all US Navy carriers, including the latest nuclear-powered ships.

The launching routine aboard a big US Navy carrier is a remarkable sight. The aircraft are brought up from the hangar on deck-edge elevators, and small tractors then "spot" them near each of four catapults, two forward and two on the angled deck extension. Bombs and rockets are brought up from the magazines by separate hoists, and aviation fuel is pumped up from tanks deep down in the ship.

The entire operation is coordinated by the "Air Boss" and his staff from the Flying Control Position or "Flyco" high up on the island superstructure. The object is to get as many aircraft airborne as possible, and so every movement on the flight deck must be carefully thought out and practiced endlessly. The various functions of the flight deck crewmen are identified by the jackets that they wear; yellow indicates the taxi-directors who direct the aircraft and purple the "grapes" who refuel the aircraft. Green is for the men who hook the aircraft to the catapult bridles and clear arrestor wires from the tail-hooks. White indicates safety, while brown denotes the "plane captains" who clean the aircraft.

Arrestor System

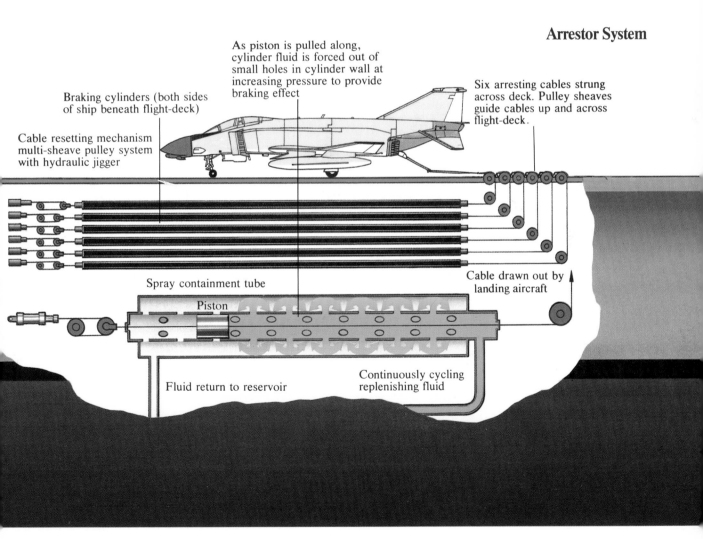

As piston is pulled along, cylinder fluid is forced out of small holes in cylinder wall at increasing pressure to provide braking effect

Six arresting cables strung across deck. Pulley sheaves guide cables up and across flight-deck.

Braking cylinders (both sides of ship beneath flight-deck)

Cable resetting mechanism multi-sheave pulley system with hydraulic jigger

Spray containment tube

Cable drawn out by landing aircraft

Piston

Fluid return to reservoir

Continuously cycling replenishing fluid

10
Helicopter Carriers and Vertical Assault

The helicopter made its debut in the Second World War, but it was too crude a machine to be effective. Not until the mid-1950s did helicopters become sufficiently reliable to serve in the front line, a fact recognized by the conversion of an old escort carrier, the USS *Thetis Bay,* into a helicopter assault ship. Almost immediately the Royal Marine Commandos tried out the concept of a helicopter-borne assault by seizing the northern end of the Suez Canal during the Anglo-French landings in Egypt in 1956.

The US Navy developed the first of a class of assault helicopter carriers (LPH) in 1959, and the British converted the carriers *Albion* and *Bulwark* for the same purpose: to get assault troops and their vehicles and guns ashore at maximum speed. Not all supplies can be carried by helicopters, and so all assault carriers are fitted with davits to carry small landing craft that can ferry heavy vehicles and supplies ashore.

The Vietnam War showed that the helicopter could provide mobility even over the worst terrain, while "gunships" could suppress enemy fire before the troops went in and even knock out armored vehicles with anti-tank missiles.

The British campaign to recapture the Falklands relied heavily on these modern techniques of "vertical assault." Both the carriers HMS *Hermes* and HMS *Invincible* are capable of accommodating Royal Marine Commandos,

although during the Falklands operations all the troop-carrying helicopters were carried by the *Hermes*.

The most advanced type of assault ship in the world is the US Navy's *Tarawa* class (LHA.15). They combine within one 40,000-ton hull all the characteristics of existing amphibious assault ships (LPHs), amphibious transport docks (LPDs), dock landing ships, and amphibious transports (AKAs).

The ships can accommodate 1900 marines as well as their support aircraft, helicopters, tanks, and vehicles. The marines can be put ashore by helicopters and by landing craft carried in a huge docking well. The ship functions like a mobile floating dock, flooding ballast tanks to allow the landing craft to leave through a huge stern gate while continuing to act as an assault carrier.

In addition to big troop-carrying helicopters, the LHAs can operate vertical takeoff AV-8A (Harrier) ground support aircraft, making them useful support carriers if the need arises.

A novel feature of the Falklands conflict was the rapid conversion of requisitioned merchant ships to operate helicopters. In addition to the container ships *Atlantic Conveyor* and *Atlantic Causeway,* other ships were hurriedly altered, one to act as an aircraft transport and others to operate anti-submarine helicopters. The luxury liner *Canberra* was given two flight decks to enable her to "cross-deck" assault troops to the amphibious ships, while the *Queen Elizabeth II* received three flight decks. These conversions also included provision for refueling and fire-fighting as well as for maintenance of the helicopters, for high-intensity operations put a great strain on helicopters and aircrew.

The Soviet Navy has shown less interest in vertical assault, but its new assault ship, the *Ivan Rogov,* is a big step forward. In addition to a large helicopter deck, the ship carries a pair of assault hovercraft in her docking well to get heavy supplies ashore without slowing down the buildup of troops ashore.

Left: Whirlwind helicopters making the world's first vertical assault at Port Said in 1956
Right: The 40,000-ton USS *Tarawa* looks like a carrier but combines the functions of dock landing ship, assault transport, and support carriers in one hull.

11 Hangar Stowage

The hangar of a modern nuclear-carrier like the *Nimitz* is a huge warehouse into which are squeezed as many as 80 aircraft at a time. Even with its wings folded, a large aircraft like the F-14 Tomcat takes up a great deal of space. Additional space is required by the maintenance men who work on the aircraft. A modern carrier must be capable of carrying out all but the most complex repairs, for the value of the aircraft carrier lies in the fact that she can operate for long periods away from her home port.

The provision of workshops and storage for aircraft spares is as important as the provision for aircraft. The *Nimitz* and her sister ships provide the equivalent of a shore air base for nine squadrons of aircraft, nearly all of different types, each requiring its own spare parts.

Aircraft are moved from the hangar to the flight deck by massive elevators. American carriers use deck-edge elevators, and the *Nimitz* class have four. The positioning of aircraft in relation to the elevators is crucial, for a rapid flow of aircraft must be maintained when a large air strike is launched. The British closed hangar did not lend itself to side-elevators, although they were tried in the *Hermes* and the previous *Ark Royal*. To cure the problem of congestion around the elevators, the new *Invincible* class carriers have a unique elevator supported by twin hydraulic arms underneath the platform. This permits aircraft to be moved around three sides, speeding up movement considerably.

The Air Group of a big American carrier varies from time to time, but a typical make-up for a *Nimitz* class nuclear-powered carrier will include F-14 Tomcat interceptors, E-2C Hawkeye airborne early warning aircraft, A-7E Corsair II strike aircraft for daytime use, A-6E Intruder strike aircraft for use in all climates, EA-6B Prowlers for

---

Below: On the starboard side of the nuclear carrier USS *Enterprise,* two of the deck-edge aircraft elevators are in the down position, while the right-hand one is nearly level with the flight deck. Aircraft are moved with wings folded to save space, and, once they reach the flight deck, they are moved rapidly to their allotted positions, or "spotted." When intensive flying operations are going on, the fresh aircraft use one set of elevators, while those being "struck down" use others.

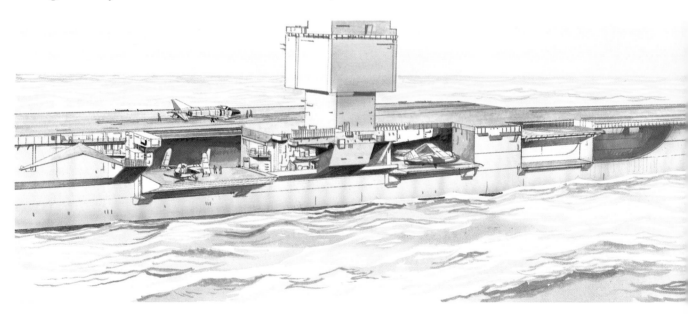

electronic warfare, S-3A Viking anti-submarine aircraft, and SH-3D Sea King anti-submarine helicopters.

The interceptors are armed with Phoenix, Sparrow, and Sidewinder missiles, as well as a 20mm Gatling gun. The Prowlers and Corsairs carry a mix of rockets, bombs, and Vulcan Gatling guns, as well as guided missiles. The anti-submarine aircraft drop sonobuoys and can attack submerged targets with depth-charges and homing torpedoes. The electronic warfare Prowlers carry powerful jammers to drown hostile radars before the strike aircraft are sent in, while the Hawkeyes carry a powerful long-range radar to track air and surface targets.

Below right: All but the highest level maintenance has to be done on board the carrier, and so the hangars and workshops must be lavishly equipped with spares and machine tools. Modern aircraft, with their complex avionics, require more maintenance than older aircraft, and the US Navy's carriers usually keep a number of aircraft parked on the flight deck in order to free part of the hangar area for essential repair work and to make it easier to move the aircraft around. The comparative spaciousness seen here suggests that almost the entire Air Group must be ranged on the flight deck or airborne.

12 Bombing Techniques

In the First World War, bombs were too small to inflict serious damage on warships. The torpedo proved a better weapon, but it was too heavy for most of the early seaplanes and landplanes. Between the two world wars, much attention was paid to high-level bombing and dive-bombing. But Second World War experience showed that the air-launched torpedo was still the most effective method of attacking ships.

Today the speed of strike aircraft rules out torpedo-attack, for torpedoes must always enter the water at the right angle and speed. For the same reason, modern jet strike aircraft cannot act as dive-bombers. There is also the problem of modern defenses, which are much more effective than they were 40 years ago. Special tactics have, therefore, been developed, such as glide-bombing. The pilot approaches in a shallow dive at high speed. Skip-bombing uses a rapid climb and turn to toss the bomb onto the target. But all techniques rely on the pilot's judgment, and experience in Vietnam showed that aircraft opposed by strong anti-aircraft fire were rarely able to hit small targets. Even more recently, the fighting around the Falklands showed that if aircraft come in low enough to bomb accurately, they become vulnerable to defensive fire, even from machine guns. Had the British ships had close-range defense, the Argentinian attackers would have suffered very heavily.

Rockets fired in salvoes are more destructive than bombs but cannot be aimed as accurately. Stand-off guided missiles are accurate but too expensive to be used in large numbers. The answer lies in a compromise: the so-called "smart" bomb, which uses a homing device to keep the bomb on course to the target.

Anti-shipping Tactics in the Falklands

During the fighting in the South Atlantic, numerous attacks were made by Argentine aircraft on the British task force. On May 12, 1982, eight A-4 Skyhawk fighter-bombers succeeded in hitting the destroyer *Glasgow* with a bomb that passed through the engine room without exploding.

A series of daring low-level attacks on May 21 sank the frigate *Ardent* and damaged the *Antrim, Argonaut, Brilliant,* and *Broadsword.* Two days later, the *Antelope* was sunk and some of the landing craft were hit. But in each case, the ships survived because the Argentine bombs failed to explode.

The reason for such a high rate of unexploded bombs was the low altitude at which the Mirages and Skyhawks were forced to fly. The concentration of fire from Rapier and Sea Dart missiles, as well as gunfire, forced the aircraft down to a point at which the bomb fuses were not designed to function — all bombs have a delay-mechanism to prevent the bomb from becoming live too soon.

One of the principal advantages of precision-guided munitions is that greater accuracy means fewer bombs to be dropped. This, in turn, makes sma¹ler demands on the carrier, which can make its ordnance stores last longer or make tradeoff in favor of a larger number of other weapons or fuel. One result in the future might be to hasten the change to V/STOL aircraft. If V/STOL aircraft such as the Harrier can extend their range by having a lighter and more effective bomb-load, they will no longer suffer so badly in comparision with fixed-wing aircraft. Increasing the speed of current V/STOL aircraft presents no technical difficulty. But for the foreseeable future, they remain poor weight-lifters. The widespread adoption of precision-guided munitions could enhance the importance of V/STOL aircraft in naval air power much more rapidly than anybody has realized. If that happens, the present upward trend in size and weight of carrier aircraft could be halted, and the growth in size of carriers, which has become their chief drawback, would be controlled.

Top left: The pre-1939 method of bombing ships was soon modified to "skip" the bomb toward the target.
Bottom left: Dive-bombing permitted more accuracy because the axis of the attacking aircraft was close to the flight path of the bomb.
Top right: "Toss bombing" allows the attacking aircraft to break away before facing defensive gunfire and missiles.
Bottom right: The "smart" bomb permits the attacker to keep clear of defensive fire while "marking" the target and guiding the bomb in flight.

V/STOL aircraft are smaller and therefore need less deck-space, use less fuel, and require less ordnance. The volume of a carrier's magazines is dictated by the number of sorties expected from the Air Group rather than the weight or number of bombs, in much the same way fuel stowage is determined.

Precision-guided munitions are guided to their target by an optical or infra-red image of the target. Some use a TV camera in the nose, and others follow a laser beam which has designated the target. Although difficult to jam, both types suffer from any form of visual interference such as smoke, fog, or dust clouds.

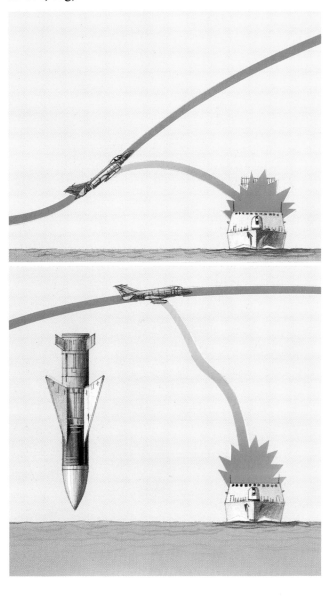

13
Missile Attacks Against Ships

The first guided missile attack against a ship was made as long ago as 1943 when the German Air Force *(Luftwaffe)* used radio-controlled glide-bombs against Allied targets. But the real age of the anti-ship missile arrived in 1967 when Egyptian missile boats sank the Israeli destroyer *Eilat* off Port Said.

France, Italy, Norway, Israel, and the United States all pushed ahead with ship-launched missiles, and out of these programs came air-launched versions of the lighter ones. The best-known of these is the AM.39 Exocet, but there are air-launched versions of the Israeli Gabriel, the Norwegian Penguin, and the American Harpoon, among others.

In a typical Exocet attack, the strike aircraft illuminates the target briefly with her radar to obtain the accurate position. This information is then put into the small computer in the missile, giving its range and bearing. When fired, the missile automatically flies down to a pre-set height,

maintaining that height by means of a radio altimeter. When it has flown about two-thirds of the way, the missile goes even closer to the water (hence the term "sea-skimmer") and switches on its own radar. This tracks in a narrow band, and, as soon as it picks up the target, the missile corrects its course to hit.

Flying close to wave-top height above the water makes a sea-skimmer very hard to detect, especially as it does not switch on its radar until it is only five or six miles away. Once its radar has locked on, the only defense is to shoot it down, either with guns or a defensive missile system such as Sea Wolf.

When the new support carrier HMS *Illustrious* was sent to the South Atlantic in June 1982 to relieve her sistership *Invincible,* she had just been given two of the latest gun systems. The multiple-barreled Vulcan Phalanx fires a stream of 20 mm bullets in a cone about 2 miles (3000 meters) away from the ship, using radar to track not only an incoming missile but the stream of bullets. This enables the cone of bullets (fired at the rate of about 3000 rounds per minute) to put a wall of lead in the path of the missile.

The Vulcan Phalanx was designed around the airborne Vulcan gun used in Vietnam. It uses revolving barrels like the old Gatling machine-gun but is driven electrically to achieve the maximum rate of fire. Although firing at the rate of 3000 rounds per minute, the Vulcan Phalanx needs only a burst lasting a second or two to achieve a kill, either by destroying the missile or by triggering off its sensitive warhead.

14
Flight Deck Layout and the Operating Cycle

The flight deck layout of a modern carrier is a direct reflection of operating procedures. In the big US Navy carriers, there are four deck-edge elevators and none on the centerline. One is on the port deck-edge, where it can bring aircraft to the pair of steam catapults in the waist of the ship. The others are forward and aft of the island on the starboard side, where they are clear of aircraft landing and those parked waiting to take off.

The hangar is divided into two bays, and, to reduce the risk of a single hit from a bomb or missile knocking out the entire hangar, each bay has to have its own elevators. Ideally each bay should have port-side and starboard-side elevators.

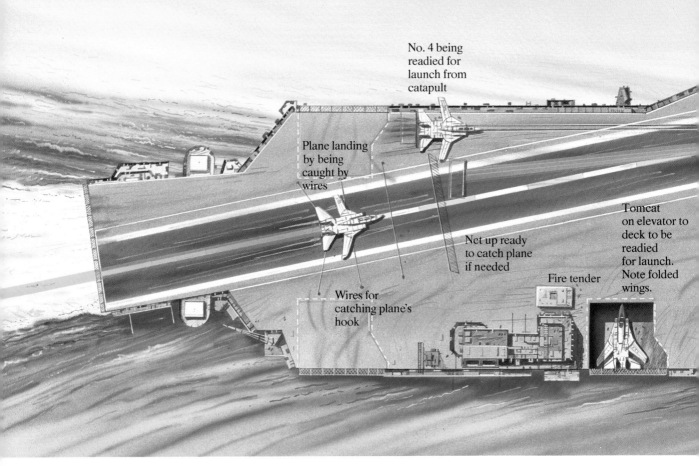

No. 4 being readied for launch from catapult

Plane landing by being caught by wires

Net up ready to catch plane if needed

Wires for catching plane's hook

Fire tender

Tomcat on elevator to deck to be readied for launch. Note folded wings.

It is necessary to have at least one port-side elevator, not only as an insurance against battle damage but also in case heavy weather restricts the use of the starboard elevators.

At the after end of the island, is a Carrier Controlled Approach (CCA) radar, providing accurate information for aircraft landing at night or in poor visibility. The CCA functions much like a ground-control radar at an airport, tracking the aircraft and marshaling them into a glide path.

The object of all carrier flying operations is to launch the maximum number of aircraft in the shortest possible time. Fuel spent flying around the carrier cuts short the endurance of the aircraft and, therefore, increases the risks. Equally, when recovering aircraft from a strike, the rate of landing is as fast as possible without endangering life.

The flight deck procedure for operating Vertical/Short Take Off and Landing (V/STOL) aircraft such as the Sea Harrier or the Russian Yak-36 *Forger* is quite different from a large carrier or CV. The basic requirement remains the same: to get the aircraft up from the hangar as fast as possible, up in the air, and back down on deck and into the hangar as fast as possible. There is, however, no need for a catapult, as the Sea Harrier can make a rolling takeoff or, in an emergency, a vertical takeoff. The rolling takeoff, either along a level flight deck or (preferably) up a Ski Jump, conserves scarce fuel, whereas the more spectacular vertical takeoff is ruinously expensive of fuel.

The other feature not required by V/STOL carriers is the arrestor wire, for the aircraft land "softly" like helicopters. However, the now-standard angled deck is still used because it provides clear deck space for marshaling aircraft waiting to take off.

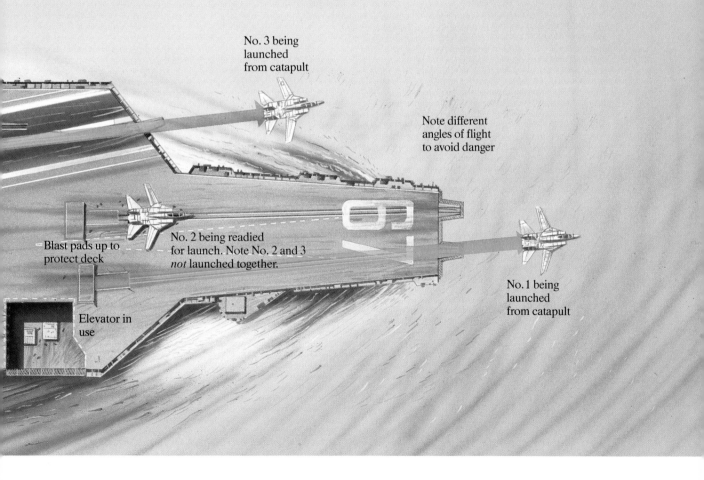

No. 3 being launched from catapult

Note different angles of flight to avoid danger

Blast pads up to protect deck

No. 2 being readied for launch. Note No. 2 and 3 *not* launched together.

No. 1 being launched from catapult

Elevator in use

15
Air Defense of a Carrier Today

A modern carrier and her aircraft together form a complete weapon system, something which is easily forgotten when assessing the carrier's chance of surviving attack.

A big carrier's defense systems extend out typically to 150 miles in the form of a Combat Air Patrol (CAP). The US Navy's F-14 Tomcat carries Phoenix air-to-air missiles, which have an extended range of 50 miles. Further in, the carrier's escorting warships form a second layer of defense with medium-range surface-to-air missiles (SAMs). The carrier herself carries Vulcan Phalanx Gatling

guns or short-range missiles to take care of any targets that leak through the two outer layers of defense.

The defense of the carrier is helped by her own radars, airborne early warning radar, and the interceptors' own radars, all of which are linked in to a computer-aided command and control system.

The defending aircraft are armed with the standard air-to-air weapons, guns and missiles, and their function is very similar to land-based interceptors. A CAP for a large carrier normally consists of four aircraft, and, as the CAP runs low on fuel, it is replaced by another group so that a constant watch is kept. The rapid reaction time of the Sea Harrier permits a variant of this, a flight deck CAP, with two Sea Harriers kept warmed up on deck. The aircraft get airborne faster because they do not need to be positioned on a catapult.

During the fighting around the Falklands, the CAPs operated by the Sea Harriers of the two carriers HMS *Hermes* and HMS *Invincible* saved the Task Force from serious damage time and time again. In all, 16 confirmed kills and one "probable" were credited to Sidewinder air-to-air missiles, four confirmed to 30 mm Aden guns, and two "probables."

When it is remembered that the entire Air Group was made up of only 28 Sea Harriers, and that on the worst day 72 Argentine aircraft attacked the ships in San Carlos Water, it is not surprising that the CAP was swamped. But, in spite of being quite outclassed for speed by the Mirages and Daggers, the Sea Harriers used their remarkable maneuverability and the AIM-9L Sidewinder missile to achieve a high degree of success.

In all, five Sea Harriers and three RAF Harriers were lost during the fighting, a remarkably low total when the intensity of the air battle is taken into account.

16 Mini-Carriers in the South Atlantic

Two large roll-on/roll-off container ships, the 15,000 tons (gross) SS *Atlantic Causeway* and her sister *Atlantic Conveyor*, were taken up by the Royal Navy in April 1982. Their primary purpose was to carry military supplies for the amphibious forces that were to recapture the Falklands, but the opportunity was taken to give both ships a limited ability to operate aircraft. Above all, both ships had to be ready by April 25, so any elaborate conversion was ruled out.

Both ships had a flush deck strengthened for carrying containers so there was no need to worry about the weight of aircraft. *Atlantic Conveyor* was earmarked to operate RAF ground-support Harriers, but her sister ship would also have to be capable of accepting the big RAF Chinook helicopters.

The solution was to stack containers on either side of the deck, providing a wind-break for the aircraft. In the *Conveyor*, there was no cover for the aircraft. But in *Causeway*, the forward containers were given a light steel roof, forming a simple hangar for the four Sea King anti-submarine helicopters.

Both ships functioned briefly as spare decks for the *Hermes* and *Invincible's* aircraft and helicopters during the operations in San Carlos Water. Like the escort carriers in the Second World War, they took some of the strain off the Task Force carriers and freed them for more important operations.

The *Atlantic Conveyor* flew off her Sea Harriers and Harriers as soon as she arrived in the Falklands, and, after the first landings, was given orders to move into San Carlos Water to fly off her Wessex and Chinook helicopters.

While moving into Falkland Sound, the Task Force was attacked by two Argentine Super Etendard strike aircraft armed with AM.39 Exocet missiles, both of which homed on the large radar echo of the *Atlantic Conveyor*. Only two minutes

after the Air Raid Warning Red, the Exocets tore into her port side, low down.

The missiles' warheads generated enormous heat and clouds of dense black smoke. Within half an hour, the fires had gotten out of control, and the Master, Captain Ian North, gave the order to abandon ship. He and 11 men died, but the rest of her crew and the naval party were rescued by nearby warships and helicopters. The burned-out wreck sank a day later.

17
Airborne ASW

The growing power of the nuclear submarine means that modern carriers have to dilute their strike aircraft with anti-submarine aircraft. For many years, the principal anti-submarine aircraft has been the helicopter, but the US Navy now operates highly specialized fixed-wing aircraft from its carriers: the S-2 Tracker and its replacement, the S-3 Viking.

The range of equipment carried by anti-submarine aircraft is impressive. Long waveband radars and infra-red seekers can detect a submarine's snorkel, while sonobuoys can be

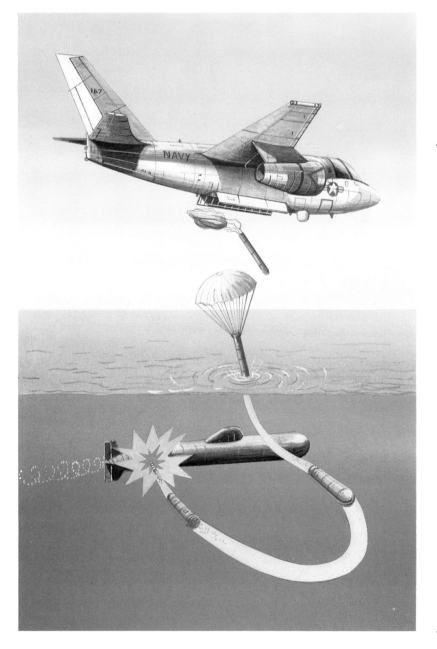

Left: The Lockheed S-3A Viking, which first flew in 1972, is the US Navy's standard carrier ASW aircraft and is unusual in being jet-powered. It can fly at 500 mph (834 km/h) and has a maximum range of almost 3,000 miles (5,000 km) at a cruising speed of 346 knots. The crew of four is made up of a pilot and co-pilot and two equipment operators in the rear cabin. The ASW equipment includes a retractable magnetic anomaly detector tail boom, a forward-looking infra-red seeker, a search radar, and various electronic counter-measures. The weapon load of the Viking is even more impressive: up to 60 sonobuoys, four MK 46 torpedoes, and two Mk 57 depth-charges. If necessary, the aircraft can be used to lay mines, and up to 1,130 kilos of stores can be carried on under-wing pylons. In spite of being a good load carrier, the Viking is compact enough for carrier operation: both the wings and the tail fin fold up.

dropped to listen for the noise of its propellers, and Magnetic Anomaly Detectors (MAD) can plot the effect of a submarine's hull on the Earth's magnetism. Once detected, the submarine can be attacked with homing torpedoes or depth-charges.

The anti-submarine helicopter performs its mission in much the same way but cannot carry as heavy a load of equipment and cannot fly as far or as fast. On the other hand, it can fly sufficiently slowly to be able to operate a dunking sonar, capable of tracking a submarine with more precision than a sonobuoy.

The value of helicopters is now so well established that modern escorts carry two of them. But the most effective way of using them at sea is in a larger ship designed to handle them. Only lack of money prevents the US Navy from building specialized anti-submarine carriers, whereas the *Invincible* class was originally designed solely to operate Sea King anti-submarine helicopters.

Right: Helicopters have been found to be one of the cheapest and most efficient methods of tracking nuclear-powered submarines. The big ASW helicopter, the Sea King, one of the largest and most advanced helicopters in the world, constitutes a complete weapons system in that it is able both to hunt and sink submarines. A Sea King helicopter uses its dipping sonar to locate a submarine, either by active "pinging" of ultrasonic echoes off the hull or by listening passively for propeller noise. Closely-spaced helicopters sending out strong signals constitute a very effective means of searching large tracts of ocean and, as the helicopter has three times the speed of the submarine, it can keep pace with the submarine if she tries to escape.

18 Airborne Early Warning

Carriers use their long-range surveillance radars and those of their interceptor aircraft to provide early warning of attacks, particularly by hostile aircraft. But both types of radar have limitations. The ship's radar is limited in its horizon (although high-flying targets can be detected at much longer ranges), and the plane's radar can only pick up targets comparatively close to the aircraft.

The solution to this problem is to raise a big surveillance radar to high altitude. This not only extends the horizon of the radar but helps to detect low-flying targets. The radar's information is passed automatically to the carrier by a data-link. Airborne Early Warning, or AEW, allows the carrier to deploy its defending interceptors more economically, as the CAP can be vectored into the correct area rather than trying to cover a full 360-degree arc.

The first carrier-borne AEW aircraft were the Avenger and Skyraider, both converted from strike aircraft. But the US Navy developed the E-1 Tracer from the S-2 Tracker anti-submarine aircraft, and the current AEW aircraft is the E-2 Hawkeye. Both aircraft have a conspicuous circular radome above the fuselage. The Hawkeye can exercise several functions. It can, for example, keep watch over a strike, sending warning of hostile aircraft before the attackers can see them. It can also control the operations of the CAP, directing individual aircraft to destroy intruders.

After operating AEW Avengers in the 1950s, the Royal Navy developed its own airborne early warning aircraft. Like the much larger E-1 Tracer, the AEW Gannet was developed from an existing anti-submarine aircraft, with an American APS-20 radar underneath the fuselage.

Using the unusual Double Mamba turboprop engine, the Gannet could stay airborne for hours, and each carrier had a flight of four.

The last AEW Gannet flight was disbanded in 1978 when the carrier *Ark Royal* was scrapped. It was hoped that in the North Atlantic, the Royal Navy could rely on shore-based AEW aircraft. But as predicted, lack of AEW aircraft put the British Sea Harriers at a great disadvantage in the Falklands. As a stop-gap, the Searchwater radar was mounted in two Sea King helicopters, the first example of helicopter-borne AEW.

The Grumman E-2 Hawkeye is, in effect, a flying radar station. It can not only detect hostile aircraft but also controls friendly aircraft, vectoring them out to intercept the enemy. Taking the radar up high extends its horizon and improves its effectiveness. The detection of incoming flights at maximum distance affords the carrier and its aircraft maximum time to react to the threat. Lack of such an aircraft or its equivalent caused the British carriers severe problems in the Falklands in 1982, and urgent steps were taken to fit Sea King helicopters with a lightweight search radar. The next development may be a V/STOL aircraft with a specially developed type of high-output radar, carrying extra fuel under the wings.

19 Carriers vs. Submarines

In the foreground is HMS *Hermes,* equipped to operate five Sea Harrier strike aircraft and nine Sea King helicopters. The aircraft and helicopters are housed in the hangar below the flight deck, where they are also maintained and repaired in elaborately equipped workshops.

Two Sea Kings are aloft, one searching for a submarine below the surface with her "dunking" sonar (left) by listening to the noise of the submarine's propeller or bouncing a supersonic pulse off its hull. The second Sea King is armed with Stingray homing torpedoes, ready to attack any contact detected by her sonobuoys. Ahead of the carrier a nuclear hunter-killer

submarine listens for any sound which will give away the enemy submarine's position.

The main defense of the *Hermes* against air or surface attack lies in her Sea Harrier vertical take-off aircraft, one of which has just flown off the flight deck using the raised ski jump at the forward end. This ramp allows the Sea Harrier to take off with a larger load of fuel or weapons.

Further defense against air attack is provided by a destroyer armed with Sea Dart guided missiles. These are aimed at aircraft which get past the defending Sea Harriers, and can shoot down supersonic aircraft at a range of 25 miles (40 km).

Beyond the destroyer is a *Broadsword* class

frigate, armed with Exocet anti-ship missiles and Sea Wolf self-defense missiles. In conjunction with the Sea Kings from the carrier, her task is to use her very long-range sonar and two Lynx helicopters to hunt for submarines.

The ASW task group receives further information from reconnaissance satellites and airborne early warning Nimrod aircraft (background).

HMS *Invincible* and her sisters, *Illustrious* and *Ark Royal,* are the world's first carriers designed from the keel up to operate vertical takeoff aircraft. The design was developed originally to provide a platform for anti-submarine helicopters to allow the projected fleet carrier *CVA.01* to carry more strike aircraft. When *CVA.01* was cancelled in 1966, the design was expanded to allow for the eventual purchase of a naval version of the Harrier V/STOL aircraft, the now famous Sea Harrier.

The primary role of the *Invincible* class is to provide anti-submarine helicopters in key checkpoints, such as the Greenland-Iceland-UK Gap, where Soviet nuclear submarines would have to pass in order to attack North Atlantic convoys. Sea Harriers are carried to fend off any surface attacks and to shoot down reconnaissance bombers, providing target-information for missile attacks. In peacetime, the air group is made up of five Sea Harriers and nine Sea Kings.

20
The Carrier Battle Group

Today the US Navy's Carrier Battle Groups are the only surface forces capable of taking the offensive against the Russian Fleet.

The basis for defending the group is that of "layers." Just as the CAP Interceptors about 14 miles (240 km) out provide an outer layer of defense against air attack, so the S-3 Vikings, using a variety of sensors, are searching for submarine contacts.

The carrier's escorts provide the second layer of defense. Missile-armed destroyers (DDGs) and cruisers (CGs) provide defense against air attack at medium range—out to 39-48 miles (65-80 km)—while their sonars are searching for submarines. If a submarine is detected, it can be attacked with homing torpedoes, either directly or from the anti-submarine helicopters carried aboard most ships.

The large number of nuclear submarines (SSNs) available now makes it possible to provide each battle group with a submarine escort, if required. A typical disposition would put the SSN ahead of the carrier, where she is well placed to spot any hostile submarine trying to ambush the carrier. If she gets left behind by a sudden alteration of course, she has sufficient margin of speed to catch up.

Aircraft or missiles which leak through the two outer layers are dealt with by close-range weapons. Unlike the carriers of the Second World War, which bristled with 20 mm and 40 mm guns, a modern US carrier is defended by, at most, three eight-cell Sea Sparrow missile launchers and four 20 mm Vulcan Phalanx Gatling guns as well as electronic jammers and chaff-launchers to decoy missiles.

The USS *Nimitz* (CVN-68) and her sister ships are the most powerful surface combatants the world has ever seen. Displacing over 96,000 tons at full load, they are driven at 33 knots by steam turbines that use steam heated by two nuclear reactors. The flight deck is 1,079 feet (327 meters)

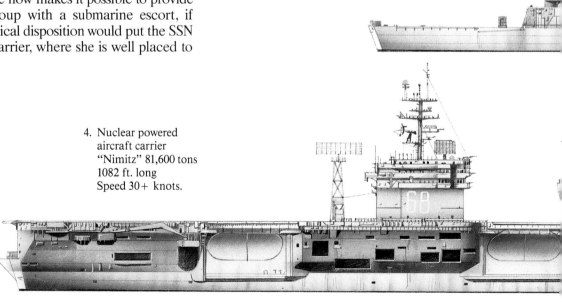

2. Cruiser "Long Beach"
   17,000 tons 721 ft. long
   missiles and guns
   speed 30 knots

4. Nuclear powered
   aircraft carrier
   "Nimitz" 81,600 tons
   1082 ft. long
   Speed 30+ knots.

long and 255 feet (77.11 m) wide and has four deck-edge aircraft elevators and four 312 foot (94.5 m) steam catapults.

Although a maximum of 100 aircraft can be carried, only 35-40 percent of them can be accommodated in the hangar. In all, some 15,000 tons of fuel, ordnance, and aviation supplies are carried. This allows them to operate continuously for 16 days. The reactor cores are expected to last 13 years—the equivalent of up to 1 million miles' steaming.

Despite frequent political attempts to abolish the carriers, they are still the most cost effective way of projecting power quickly, and the *Nimitz* has been followed by the *Dwight D. Eisenhower* and *Carl Vinson*. Three more, the *Theodore Roosevelt* (CVN-71), the *George Washington*, and the *Abraham Lincoln,* are under construction.

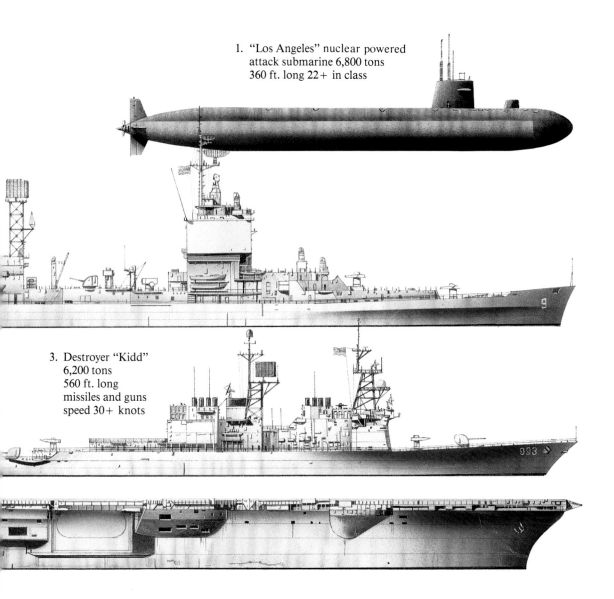

1. "Los Angeles" nuclear powered
   attack submarine 6,800 tons
   360 ft. long 22+ in class

3. Destroyer "Kidd"
   6,200 tons
   560 ft. long
   missiles and guns
   speed 30+ knots

Glossary

ACV
US Navy designation for Aircraft Transport (formerly AVG)

AIR GROUP
A term embracing the aircraft and all related personnel, including aircrew, flight deck handlers, maintainers, and command staff, embarked on an aircraft carrier

ACCELERATOR
Royal Navy term for a catapult-type device which accelerated the aircraft to its takeoff speed, to be distinguished from a catapult which launched the aircraft at higher speed

ASDIC
British-designed underwater ultra-sonic device for detecting submarines (replaced in 1948 by US equivalent "Sonar")

AVGAS
Acronym for Aviation Gasoline, the high-octane fuel used in piston-engined aircraft. Replaced by kerosene-based fuels when turbojets became commonplace.

AVG
US Navy designation for Aircraft Transport (replacing ACV)

AAW
Acronym for Anti-Air Warfare, a modern term which embraces fleet air defense by missiles and guns

ARRESTING GEAR
Term which includes wires for slowing down aircraft landings, the recuperators, and safety barriers

ARRESTOR WIRE
Cable arranged at 90 degrees to axis of flight deck, designed to engage the tailhook of the aircraft during landing

ASW
Acronym for Anti-Submarine Warfare, a term including all methods of attacking submarines

ANGLED DECK
Arrangement of the flight deck in modern carriers, with the axis skewed to port, enlarging the useable area of the deck and permitting aircraft to overshoot safely if they miss the arrestor wires on landing

BAVG
British Aircraft Transport, early US Navy designation for AVGs or escort carriers earmarked for Britain under Lend-Lease

BATTLESHIP
An armored warship relying on heavy-caliber guns as her main offensive weapons

BATSMAN
Nickname for the Landing Control Officer, who used two paddles (handlamps at night) to show the incoming pilot whether his approach was correct for height and angle (replaced by landing sights)

BOMB LIFT
Small elevator used to carry ordnance from magazines to hangar or flight deck, for loading aircraft

BOMBERS
In early carriers these were formerly divided into dive-bombers and torpedo-bombers, but in modern carriers bomb- and rocket- carrying aircraft are called "strike" or "support" aircraft. "Strategic" bombers were formerly carried in US carriers to deliver nuclear weapons against land-targets.

CCA
Carrier Controlled Approach radar, used to track and direct aircraft coming in to land

CV
US Navy designation for aircraft carrier (originally to distinguish from CA, "armored cruiser")

CVA
Attack Carrier indicating that she carries bombers and fighter squadrons

CVAN, CVN
Nuclear-powered versions of the CVA and CV

CVE
Escort carrier

CVS
Support Carrier, indicating that she carries anti-submarine aircraft

CVL
Light Carrier

CAM-ships
Catapult-Armed Merchant Ships, tramp steamers given a hydraulic catapult on the forecastle, enabling them to launch a Hurricane fighter to defend against attacks by German bombers

CANTED DECK
Original US Navy term for angled deck

CATWALK
Walkway at edge of flight deck to enable personnel to take shelter during landing and takeoff of aircraft

CLOSED HANGAR
A hangar surrounded by workshops and other working spaces, with no direct access to the open air

DAMAGE CONTROL
The organization and equipment of personnel on board a warship, specifically trained to restrict damage, whether from enemy action or accident

ELEVATOR
Large hoist used to transfer aircraft between the hangar and flight deck; they fall into two types, deck-edge or centerline

FLOATPLANE
Modern term for a seaplane, a conventional airframe equipped with floats to allow it to land and take off from water

FLIGHT DECK
Any clear area of deck dedicated to the launch and recovery of aircraft; carriers have full-length flight decks, whereas other warships have small flight decks, usually aft

FDO
Fighter Direction Officer, in Second World War carriers officer responsible for controlling the movements of defending fighters during an enemy attack

FLYCO
The Flying Control position; an extension of the bridge designed to give a clear view of the flight deck, from which the Commander, Air, and his staff control all flying operations

FLEET CARRIER
Obsolete term for the largest carriers from the fact that they operated with the main fleet, rather than on subsidiary duties, hence Light Fleet Carrier

GOOFERS' GALLERY
Naval slang for a walkway on the island superstructure, from which anyone not permitted on the flight deck or in the flyco can watch proceedings in safety

HYDRO-AEROPLANE
Original term for seaplane and floatplane (officially banned by Winston Churchill in early days of Royal Naval Air Service as too cumbersome)

HANGAR
Enclosed area for storing aircraft to protect them from damage, hence hangar deck, etc.

HELICOPTER CARRIER
Usually a smaller ship, equipped only to operate rotary-wing aircraft, having a lightly stressed deck and no catapults or arrestor wires. The ability of V/STOL aircraft to make "soft" landings enables them to use helicopter carriers as well.

HURRICANE BOW
US Navy term for what was standard in British carriers, a fully enclosed bow which prevents water and spray from finding its way inside the ship in heavy weather.

Index

ISLAND
Narrow superstructure accommodating a carrier's bridge, controls, and funnel uptakes. Although early designs used the port side, and the Japanese tried port-side islands in the 1930s, the starboard side is now standard.

JATO
Jet Assisted Take Off; a system of auxiliary rockets used to speed up launching of piston-engined aircraft (late Second World War through 1950s)

LANDING SIGHT
Optical device to assist pilots in judging their landing approach, the modern equivalent of the "batsman"

LIGHT FLEET CARRIER
A small carrier capable of operating strike and interceptor aircraft, supplementing the larger "fleet" carriers (a Second World War expedient)

MAC-SHIPS
Merchant Aircraft Carriers, British grain-carriers, and oil-tankers converted into escort carriers by the addition of a light flight deck. They differed from escort carriers in retaining their cargo-carrying capacity and in being civilian-manned.

OPEN HANGAR
A hangar whose sides are open to the outside air (although the large openings can be closed by roller shutters)

ROUND-DOWN
The sloped after end of the flight deck, designed to facilitate safer landings if aircraft landed "short." No longer important, thanks to angled decks and arrestor gear

RATOG
Rocket Assisted Take Off Gear, the British name for JATO

SEA CONTROL SHIP
An "austere" design of US Navy carrier, intended to operate ASW helicopters and Harrier VSTOL aircraft to supplement the main carrier forces in securing "sea control" rather than seeking battle with the enemy's main forces

STOL
Acronym for Short Take Off and Landing; strictly speaking, all carrier aircraft are STOL types with elaborate means of slowing down landing speeds as well as catapult-launching

STOVL
Short Take Off and Vertical Landing; the correct term for aircraft of the Harrier and Sea Harrier type, which need a short "rolling" takeoff to be able to carry a normal payload and then land vertically like a helicopter

STEAM CATAPULT
Device for launching aircraft, using steam from the ship's boilers or her nuclear heat-exchanger. It replaced earlier hydraulic, pneumatic, or cordite-powered types, being able to take the extra weight of modern aircraft.

TASK FORCE
Term introduced by the US Navy to cover any large formation of ships not based on the main fleet of battleships and now widely used to cover any group based on a carrier

TASK GROUP
A detachment from a Task Force, essentially a part of the main force, irrespective of size

THROUGH DECK
A long-winded term for a full-length flight deck, used as a device by the Royal Navy in the 1970s to avoid political criticism of their plans to build a ship capable of operating STOVL aircraft

VERTICAL ASSAULT
Amphibious landings by means of helicopters instead of landing aircraft

VSTOL
Acronym for Vertical or Short Take Off and Landing, the popular term but not as accurate as STOVL